ROCKY MOUNTAIN SEASONS

From Valley to Mountaintop

by Diane L. Burns

photographs by
Kent and Donna Dannen

MACMILLAN PUBLISHING COMPANY · NEW YORK

MAXWELL MACMILLAN CANADA · TORONTO

MAXWELL MACMILLAN INTERNATIONAL
NEW YORK · OXFORD · SINGAPORE · SYDNEY

In some ways, mountains and people are alike.
The way people look can change from day to day.
A mountain's appearance changes, too, with quick-lived
    weather:
a snowstorm, cheery sunshine, a whispering wind.
All these can come and go.
Slowly, over time, man and the elements—
water, wind, heat, and cold—
make other, gradual changes in how the mountains look.

The wild mountains of the Rockies
appear different in different seasons of the year.
Spring arrives on a softening winter wind.
With the air warming and cooling by turn,
ledges and slopes slowly lose their snowy blanket.
Melting ice spills into creeks, which swell and join other creeks
flowing down the mountain toward the valleys.
Along the way, they awaken and nourish the ground.

What awakens sleeping wild creatures?
The drip, drip of melting snow?
Pale sunlight slanting across the doorway of a burrow?
Perhaps the whispering spring wind calls to them.
Or perhaps the creature's own body knows when it is time.

All mountain creatures greet springtime eagerly.
Newly born animals arrive with bright eyes and unsure steps.
Green shoots poke above ground, making mountain meadows
thick and soft.

Animals that wintered in sheltered bottomlands
begin upward travel toward the peak.
Those that spent the winter in other, warmer places
return to the high country.

Streams and creek banks become noisy with new life:
Insects sing loud choruses;
birds chatter together.
In the mud of wet places, animal tracks show many struggles
of life and death.

In late spring, some of the swollen creeks
settle into a steady flow.
Others dry up until the next springtime.
A few stubborn patches of snow
cling to cool, dark places around rocks and trees.
These patches remain year-round.

In summer, the high country becomes a paint box of color.
Green meadows,
damp fringes around springs and creeks, and
even rocky places
glow with wildflowers.

A mountain summer is gaily colored,
but also short and busy.
All creatures on the mountain grow and grow.
Young animals play and chase.
Lambs and kids bound up and down steep, rocky slopes,
coyote pups tussle,
fledglings try their wings.
Day by day, they grow stronger in the skills
that help them survive.

In the summertime, a mountain wind has many voices.
It whispers through feathery pines and meadow grasses
and chuckles around rock piles.
Sometimes, in stormy weather, summer wind roars through
mountain valleys like a runaway train.
At other times, summer wind chatters across barren ground
at the mountain's very top,
sounding as if people are talking and laughing together.

A summer mountain's face changes often.
Clouds dance in weather-telling patterns.
Cottonball clouds bring sunny skies,
wispy ponytail clouds warn of changing weather,
lumpy clouds hanging like gray balloons mean thunder
    and lightning
are coming—now!

On summertime mountains, severe weather
can wrap the high country in an icy coat.
Hail may pound the mountaintop
while rain drenches the lower slopes
and clogs the valleys with clouds.
A blizzard may come
with howling winds and snowdrifts.

Then, as quickly as it came, the storm moves on,
stringing a rainbow-necklace between the mountain and the sky.
Sunshine warms the freezing air,
melts the glittering hail and ice,
and summer returns again.

Summer sunsets come late,
splashing rose and cream and purple
until darkness covers all the sky and the land.
Then the huge moon rises, and rocks and trees
on the mountain form shadowy shapes beneath it.

The night sky seems to burst open with stars.
In the darkness,
the mountain creatures hunt or are hunted.
Creatures of the night seek their food,
gliding on silent wings,
stalking on padded feet.
The hunted ones become shadows,
silent as a thought,
swift as a breath.

As summer dries into autumn,
grasses become tinder-dry.
Dead trees, standing like huge matchsticks, ignite
with the spark from a lightning bolt.
Wildfire!
Smoke and flames send animals scurrying to find
safe new homes away from the heat.
Afterwards, the burned area seems dead.
But it isn't. Like human skin,
a mountain's wound can heal.

The heat opens thickly overgrown areas to new growth.
Many mountain animals and birds
eat the tender new plants that spring up.
Sometimes autumn arrives
with the scent of wood smoke still hanging in the
high country air.

Autumn is a time of gathering on the mountain.
As days become shorter in the highest places,
animals gather the last of the season's wild foods—
nuts, grasses, seeds, berries, roots.

Bears and other animals,
and birds, such as hawks and owls, hunt extra meals
to store up fat against the harsh winter months ahead.

Autumn is mating season.
Males gather with the females,
to whom young will be born the next spring.

Autumn is also a time of scattering.
Riding piggyback on the chilly wind,
or clinging to the feet and fur of animals,
seeds find new homes.
Some seeds are eaten, then left behind in droppings
on another part of the mountain.

Some animals and songbirds scatter to warmer
climates, because weather in this season of
gathering and scattering becomes colder and colder.

The winter wind has a giant's voice.
It moans and howls day and night.
Snowstorms come and go on that wind.
Not much stands against it. Small animals
snuggle underground or burrow deep within rocky spaces
and tree trunks.

Larger animals—elk and sheep—seek lower valleys
where they are sheltered from the stormy blasts
while they search for food and water.

Some animals brave the windy peak,
their bodies especially made for this season.
Thick fur protects rabbits, wildcats, and others from the cold
and wide feet help them travel; their tracks
stitch patterns across the quilt of snow.

From winter to winter, a mountain wind
carves rocks and trees with a strong hand.
Snow and ice help shape the landscape.
Pillars of snow stretch toward the sky.
Towering ice castles shimmer in the cold winter sun.
Huge waves of snow ripple across mountain meadows
and pile up in mammoth drifts.
During winter months,
the high country sleeps beneath a blanket of snow,
waiting for new seasons of change
to begin again.
Each day, weather causes short-lived changes
in the high country.
Spring to winter and back again,
longer-lasting changes come with
winds and heat and cold—and man—
season after season,
in the wild Rocky Mountains.

To the memory of Bobbie McCoy, Cobalt Fire/Recreation Guard,
who first opened my heart to the wonders of Middlefork Peak Lookout,
especially its bluebirds
—D.B.

For Patrick
—K. & D. D.

GUIDE TO PHOTOGRAPHS

RMP = Rocky Mountains National Park, Colorado; YP = Yellowstone National Park, Wyoming. *Title page,* bighorn sheep grazing, Longs Peak in background, RMP; *page 2,* Longs Peak, RMP; *page 3,* eroded walls of the Grand Canyon of the Yellowstone River, YP; *page 4,* Roaring River, RMP; *page 5,* yellow-bellied marmot emerging from den; *page 6,* elk in river valley, YP; *page 7,* elk on alpine tundra, RMP; *page 8,* left—wolf, right—raccoon; *page 9,* snow in summer, Timberline Falls, RMP; *page 10* (inset), arnica, paintbrush, bistort, asters, and golden ragwort by creek; *pages 10-11,* alpine tundra meadow, RMP; *page 12,* mountain goat kid; *page 13,* fledgling broad-tailed hummingbird; *page 14,* wind-shaped limber pine, RMP; *page 15,* top—cumulus clouds, bottom—thunder clouds; *page 16,* left—alpine sunflower in summer snow, right—subalpine fir in summer storm; *page 17,* rainbow over Prospect Mountain, Estes Park, Colorado; *pages 18-19,* Trail Ridge, RMP; *page 20,* forest fire; *page 21,* top—fireweed in burned forest, bottom—mule deer grazing on new growth; *page 22,* top—least chipmunk, bottom—red squirrel's cache of lodgepole pine cones; *page 23,* top—black bear, bottom—great horned owl; *page 24,* cow and bull moose; *page 25,* left—wild grasses, right—male mountain bluebird; *page 26,* Grand Teton National Park, Wyoming; *page 27,* bull elk; *page 28,* cougar; *page 29,* top—snowshoe hare tracks, bottom—winter plumage of white-tailed ptarmigan; *page 30* (inset), ice on queen's crown; *pages 30-31,* wind-sculpted snow.

Macmillan Publishing Company is part of the Maxwell Communication Group of Companies.
Macmillan Publishing Company, 866 Third Avenue, New York, NY 10022.
Maxwell Macmillan Canada, Inc., 1200 Eglinton Avenue East, Suite 200, Don Mills, Ontario M3C 3N1
First edition. Printed in the United States of America.

10 9 8 7 6 5 4 3 2 1

The text of this book is set in 14 point Palatino. Book design by Constance Ftera.

Library of Congress Cataloging-in-Publication Data
Burns, Diane L. Rocky Mountain seasons : from valley to mountaintop / by Diane L. Burns ; photographs by Kent and Donna Dannen. — 1st ed.   p.   cm.   Summary: Text and photographs provide a look at changes that occur in the landscape and animals of the Rocky Mountains during each season.   ISBN 0-02-716142-0   1. Natural history—Rocky Mountains—Outdoor books—Juvenile literature. 2. Seasons—Rocky Mountains—Juvenile literature. [1. Natural history—Rocky Mountains. 2. Seasons. 3. Rocky Mountains—Description and travel.] I. Dannen, Kent, ill. II. Dannen, Donna, ill. III. Title. QH104.5.R6B87 1993
508.78—dc20   92-22833